Google account befor
setup process.

MW00960436

Next, your app will decide if Google Home can have access to your personal information, like your notes, calendar, and so on. This helps Google give you the best results with certain commands, such as asking what you have to do today. Know that everybody that is within speaking range of your device can access this sort of information. With this step, you can pick "Skip" or "Allow" to continue.

Next, you will set your location and allow Google to access this information. The app will then try to locate where you are. If it turns out to be off, you can select the pencil icon and type in your location. After you have entered in your location, select "Set Location."

Next, you will be asked if you what to receive e-mail notifications on current events and information about your Google Home. Use the toggle switch to turn it on or off and then continue with the setup.

The next step is to pick your music streaming provider. YouTube and Google Play Music will be options, but you are also able to link Pandora or Spotify. With Spotify, you have to have a premium account to use it. Once done, select continue.

Once you do this, you will likely receive a message that tells you your Google Home is updating, sit back a little bit and allow it to finish.

After the updating is done, you will need to reboot the device. Select "Reboot."

After it reboots, the app will tell you that setup has finished. Select "Continue" then you can choose to continue with the tutorial, or skip the tutorial.

Your device is now set up, and you are ready to explore all the things you can with your new Google Home.

Google Home

Ultimate Guide to Quickstart Your Google Home Experience

Kyle Black

will be able to use your new Google Home in no time.

Thanks for choosing this book. Let's begin learning about Google Home so you can start impressing your friends today.

Google Home Setup

If you haven't heard, Google Home is another Wi-Fi speaker and can help you control your smarthome devices. It can also act as a family assistant. It can be used to play a variety of entertainment options, manage your daily tasks, and a faster way to find answers to your questions.

You can get various bases for your Google Home so that it matches your décor. Underneath the shell is the speaker that will make your life so much easier. That's where you Google Assistant lives.

On top of your device, you will find four LEDs, which is a capacitive touch display. This will be what you touch to interact with your device. There aren't any buttons on top of the device, but you will find a mute button on the shell. Google Home can tell the difference between voice and noise.

With Google Home, you will have control over audio and music playback, smart home devices, Google search, and many other helpful features. Before you can begin experimenting with what you can do with your Google Home, you have to get it set up first.

It only takes a few minutes to get your Google Home set up. After you plug in the device, it automatically begins to boot up. After that, you will have to have the app on your phone to finish the setup. You can get this app for any Android or iOS device.

Once you have downloaded the app, open the app and select the "Accept" button that will show on the bottom-right corner.

The app will soon let you know that it has found your Google Home device. Select "Continue" to start the setup.

Once the app has connected to your Google Home, your device will start playing a test to make sure it is connected. Select "Play Test Sound" once it pops up to start the process.

When you hear your Google Home play the test sound, select "I Heard the Sound" on the device. If you don't hear anything, select "Try Again."

Once the setup continues, you will have to pick the room that your device will be located. Choose "Select a room" and then pick the room your device is in. Then select "Continue" once done.

The next step is to connect your Google Home to a Wi-Fi network. Choose "Select a Wi-Fi network" and then select your Wi-Fi from the list. If needed, enter your password and then continue.

After your device is connected to your Wi-Fi, you need to select "Sign In."

If you are logged into other Google apps, then your account should pop up with the choice to sign in. Select "Continue as [your name]." If you don't see that, you will have to sign into your

Contents

Introduction

Amazon Echo has been dominating the voice activated speaker market for a long time now, but now there's Google Home. Google Home offers much of the same features along with some even better ones. Learning how to use this kind of technology can be quite confusing, especially with the technological mumbo-jumbo that comes in the box. Luckily for you, you have this book.

Having Google Home gives you the ability to do millions of fun and amazing things. You can amaze your friends by controlling things in your house with just your voice, but you can't do that if you don't know how.

In this book, you will find an understandable overview of how to use your Google Home effectively. It will cover the basic setup, h setup apps, how to use its audio featureou set timers, reminders, and many mor

App Features

To control and program your Google Home device, you will have to download The Google Home app. You may have already used this app if you have any Chromecast devices, which includes speakers or TV with Chromecast built-in, Chromecast audio, and Chromecast Ultra. The app used to go by the name Google Cast, so you may even already have it downloaded.

Not only does it control your Chromecast devices, but it also controls your Google Home device, and helps you to discover new content.

When you are on your Google Home app you will find:

- Search

This allows you to search for the content that you have on all of your apps. This feature only works in the US.

- Discover tab

This will show different things that you can do with your device and apps. It also shows you new features that are available. You will have access to more than 1000 apps, and the latest tips, features, and offers.

- Listen tab

This is where you go to locate audio that you have on apps you already have installed.

- Watch tab

This is where you find the movies and TV shows that you have from apps that you already have installed. This works for Chromecast TVs and Chromecast only. You will also see what all is trending on your apps, such as Google Play Movies, YouTube, Hulu, Netflix, and HBO Now.

- Devices

This is where you go to see all the Google Home and Chromecast devices you have. It is also where you manage these devices as well.

- Setup

This is where you go to setup a new device that you have.

Depending on the Chromecast and Google Home devices you have, these tabs may change. You will only see things that correspond with the devices you have.

To begin a setup for a new device, you can click the Devices icon at the top right of the app. This will begin the setup process as we covered in the first chapter. This is also where you can go to control playback and adjust your backdrop settings for your TV, and much more.

Device Cards

When you click on the devices icon, the one icon in the top right corner, you will find these cards to help you create the best experience possible with your Google Home and Chromecast devices.

- New Device Card

When your app finds a new device nearby, this card will appear. This is where you will find the setup tab to begin the setup of a new device. You even have the option to ignore a device card if you're not interested in setting up the device in the present moment.

- Ready to Cast

This will show you the devices that you have that have already been setup and are ready for use.

- Active Device

This shows your devices that you already have setup and are currently running. This is where you will find what is currently playing, and where you control the volume and playback.

- Linked Devices

This will show you all the devices that are linked to your account that gives you features that you can customize, like voice control, and backdrop.

- Ignored Devices

This is where you can find devices that you have ignored. To find this card, scroll to the very bottom of your Home screen and select Ignored New Devices. The available devices that you are close to will show up, and then you can choose the device that you want to setup.

Discover

- Live Cards

With your Google Home devices, this card will help you configure features and complete certain actions.

- Offer Card

This is where you will see offers and promotions for apps that have and have not been installed. All you have to do is select the card to receive the offer. You can also press the three dots in the top right corner of the card to view all offers, hide terms, redeem, and select.

- App Cards

This is where you will find Chromecast-enabled games, apps, and more that you don't have yet. Select "Open App" if you are interested in downloading.

- Feature Cards

For Google Home devices, this card will give you tips to make your Google Home experience amazing.

- Collection Cards

This is where you will find a collection of cards or apps like music apps.

Personalization

- Feeds

In your Listen and Watch tabs, you will get recommendations for TV shows, podcasts, music, and more based on the things that you have already watched or listened to.

- Offers

In your Watch tab, you will find offers based on what you have been doing or the things that you are interested in.

- Shelf Titles

You will also get a "Recommended for you" content that the app has based on your interests and activities. There will also be a "Featured/Popular/Trending" shelf that is based on what other people have been watching.

- App launcher

If you scroll all the way to the bottom, you will discover a list of your Chromecast-enabled apps that you have installed on your tablet or phone.

- Browse

If you swipe left, you will see details about certain content, which can include trailers or reviews. This feature is only on Android devices.

Google Home Features

Your Google Home device offers lots of features. New ones are being added almost all the time. To give you an idea of what you can do with your Google Home device, here is a breakdown of some of its features.

Have Fun

With these features, you will get to have fun with your assistant. Use these when you want to lighten up the day. You can test your trivia smarts, listen to jokes, and play other games with your Google Home.

- Delight

Have fun by asking you Google Home some questions. Whenever you want a little fun, say "Hey Google," and then ask it a question, or simply say "Entertain me."

- Easter eggs

Your Google Home is full of surprises, so when you want to discover something new, start by saying "Hey Google," and then ask "What are your Easter eggs?"

- Games

You can also play games with you Google Home. As always, begin by saying "Hey Google" after that you can pick a game. Some options are mad libs, crystal ball, and play lucky trivia. Some more options are to ask you device to sing a song.

Control Your Home

Your Google Home has the ability to control any smart home devices you have. You can set it up to control your lights, thermostat, and many other things. We will discuss most of these in more depth later.

- IFTTT (If This, Then That)

You can make your own commands for your Google Home by using IFTTT. This is a separate company that can help you expand the capabilities of your device. An example of this would be if you said "I'm going to be late", a text would be sent to your family so that they would know.

- Light control

If you have Philips Hue or SmartThings, you can control your lights with your Google Home. By simply saying "Turn on [light name]" you can turn on lights in your house without flipping a switch.

- Smart plugs and switch control

You can control Belkin Wemo switches or plugs, and any switches that are connected to SmartThings, with your Google Home.

- Thermostat control

If you have a thermostat connected to SmartThings, Honeywell Thermostat, or a Nest Thermostat, you can control the temperature in your house with you Google Home. You can switch between cooling and heating modes and more.

Plan Your Day

With you Google Home you will be able to control your tasks for the day with your voice. Having it connected to your calendar makes your life a lot easier.

- Calendar

After you allow your Google Home to have access to your information, you can ask your device what is on your schedule for the day. You can ask about a certain event, or ask for everything on a certain day.

- Flight information

You can ask for updates and information about a flight that you have coming up. Some things you could as are, "Is my flight on time?" or "Is my flight delayed?" along with many other things.

- Local guide

Google Home can give you information about places around town. Ask for the hours of operation for a restaurant, or find out the address to a shop.

- My day

Each morning you can ask your Google Home to give you a quick overview of what your day will look like. This snippet will include news, reminder, commute, calendar, and weather.

- Traffic

You can quickly ask about current traffic and travel time for biking, walking, and driving.

- Weather

You can quickly find out how the weather for the day looks by asking your Google Home. It can also tell you how the upcoming week looks.

Manage Tasks

Google Home works like a personal assistant. It can be used to take care of many tasks that you may have to keep up with during the day.

- Alarm

With your Google Home, you can set, snooze, stop, cancel, and check several alarms.

- Car service

You can access Uber with your Google Home. Ask Google Home "Call and Uber," and you will have a ride in a few minutes.

- Shopping list

You can ask your Google Home to add items to your shopping list that you can access later on your phone. You can also ask what is already on it.

- Timer

Google Home can cancel, resume, check, pause, and set timers.

Get Answers

You Google Home gives you access to Google 24/7 without having to use your phone or a computer to find answers to your questions.

- Calculator

You can use your device to answer math problems that you can't seem to figure out.

- Dictionary

Quickly figure out the correct spelling and definition of a word.

- Facts & Info

You can quickly find out the answer to a question you may have.

- Finance

You can ask about stock prices, and other information about the stock market you may have.

- Learn more

You can find out what other things you can do on your Google Home by asking your Google Home.

- Nutrition

If you're wondering about nutritional facts concerning a certain food, Google Home can answer those questions.

- Sports

You can get live updates for a sports game. You can also find out when the next game is and where.

- Translation

You can translate phrases or words to a language that you understand.

Entertainment

You're Google Home gives you access to several entertainment options without having to touch anything.

- Audio streaming

You can stream audio to your device from your phone with the use of over a hundred apps.

- Multi-room audio

You can connect any Chromecast built-in speakers, Chromecast audio, and Google Home devices together so that you can have the same music all throughout your house.

- Music

You can play music from all types of services based on activity, mood, playlist, album, genre, song, or artist.

- News

You can quickly find out the latest news from sources that you actually trust.

- Podcasts

You can easily listen to your podcasts on your Google Home device.

- Radio

Just like with podcasts, you can listen to radio shows as well.

- Speaker streaming

You can stream any type of audio to a speaker that is connected with Chromecast built-in or Chromecast audio plugged in.

- TV streaming

Just like with speakers, you can stream video to TVs that have Chromecast.

Podcasts and Shows

You can use Google Home to listen to shows and podcasts anywhere in your house without the need for a handheld device.

At the moment, Google Home doesn't support request podcasts from partner players, such as TuneIn, Google Play Music, and Spotify. This means you can't say "Hey Google, play my podcast on TuneIn." However, you can say, "Hey Google, play [podcast] podcast."

Control Your Shows

These are some examples of ways to communicate with your Assistant with your Google Home when you want to listen to your favorite shows and podcasts.

Every time you want to tell you Google Home to do something, always begin by saying "Ok Google," or "Hey Google." That means for everything you see in this book in quotation marks, make sure you place "Ok Google" or "Hey Google" in front of them.

- To be able to listen to a podcast you can say: "Listen to Savage Lovecast," or "Play The Heart podcast."

- To finish listening to a podcast say: "Continue listening to The Heart."

- To play the latest episodes of a podcast say: "Play the latest episode of Savage Lovecast."

- To listen to the previous or next episode say: "Previous," or "Next episode."

- To pause a podcast, say: "Pause the podcast."

- To resume playing the podcast say: "Resume."

- To stop playing the podcast say: "Stop podcast."

- To play the next or previous podcast say: "Next podcast," "Previous podcast," "Skip," "Previous," or "Next."

- To find out what podcast is playing say: "What podcast is being played?"

At the moment, podcasts aren't actually listed in the app. Just ask you device to play a podcast and it will. You can also talk to your Assistant while a show or podcast is playing. When you ask a question, the show will pause, and then resume once the question has been answered.

Different Ways

You can also control the playback of your podcast with your Google Home device.

- To play, pause, or stop your podcast, tap the top of your device once.

- To increase the volume of your podcast, swipe the top of your device in a clockwise motion.

- To decrease the volume of your podcast, swipe the top of your device in a counterclockwise motion.

- To begin your request, press the top of your device, holding it until you are done.

You can also control your podcast and shows through the app on your phone or tablet.

- Your tablet or phone needs to be connected to the Wi-Fi that your device is connected with.

- Open up the app on your tablet or phone.

- Press the devices icon in the upper right corner of the home screen.

- Scroll until you find the card that is associated with the device that is playing your podcast.

- The card will show you the title and current season of the podcast being listened to.

- From here you can adjust the volume, resume, pause, and stop your podcast.

Using Android Audio

With your Google Home device, you can play all your favorite music, podcasts, playlists, and more from your Android phone or tablet. This is what is referred to as mirroring.

Make you pay attention to these important factors:

- You can only cast audio from and Android device that runs Android 4.4.2 or higher.

- Make sure that your "Power Saving Mode" isn't on. This has the ability limit the processing power which may end up affect how the cast features perform.

- You have to have "Microphone" permission turn on in your Google Play Services app for you to successfully cast with Chromecast Audio. If this isn't on, then the session will automatically disconnect as soon as you try to connect.

- o To change the permission:

  - Tap the settings icon on your Android device.

  - Scroll and select Apps>Google Play Services>Permissions

  - Find "Microphone" and set the slider to on

Cast Your Audio

The first step is to cast your Android Audio from your device.

1. Your device needs to be connected to the same Wi-Fi as your Google Home.

2. Open up your Google Home app.

3. Select the menu icon in the upper left corner. Then select "Cast Screen/Audio", then "Cast Screen/Audio".

4. Choose your Google Home device.

5. Then begin playing your audio content.

The second step is to control your audio with voice commands.

It's important to know that the commands that are used to play media cannot be used when you are trying to play Android Audio on your Google Home.

- To stop the audio that is playing say: "Stop."

- To adjust the volume of the audio, say: "Max volume," or "Turn it up / down."

Here are some more commands to help you to control the volume of your audio.

- To turn up the volume, say: "Turn it up, " and Google Home will turn up the volume by 10%.

- To turn down the volume, say: "Turn it down, " and Google Home will turn down the volume by 10%.

- To set a specific level for your volume, say: "Volume to 75%" or "Volume level three" and Google Home will set the volume to the specific level you asked.

- To set to max volume, say "Max volume, " and Google Home will set the volume to 10.

- To set to a minimum volume, say "Minimum volume, " and Google Home will set the volume to 1.

- To change the level by a certain amount, say "Decrease volume by 20%" or Increase volume by 30%" and Google Home will change the volume by the specific amount.

- To hear what level the volume is set at, say "What's the volume?" and Google Home will tell you what the volume level is.

You can control the volume of your Google Home when music is or isn't playing. If you change the volume when audio isn't playing, you will hear a confirmation from your Google Home.

If you want to stop casting Android audio, here is how to do so:

Notification drawer:

1. Pull the notification drop-down open on your device.

2. Select the disconnect icon on the bar.

App:

1. Open up your Google Home app.

2. Select the menu icon, then "Cast Screen/Audio", and then select disconnect.

How to Use Guest Mode

You Google Home has a guest mode that you can use when you have friends over that would like to cast their music to your device. This is especially helpful when you are having a party. They can cast their media to your Google Home without having to connect to your Wi-Fi, and this works for Android and iOS devices.

First, the host must set up the guest mode.

You, the host, can make your password private. Your guests will be able to cast their media as long as they stay in the room that houses your Google Home.

How to set up your guest mode:

1. As always, your tablet or phone and your Google Home all need to be connected to the same Wi-Fi network.

2. Open up your Google Home app.

3. Select the devices icon in the top right corner to find Google Home device that is available.

4. If you are not already, sign into your Google account.

5. Once you found the device that you want to set to guest mode, select the three vertical dots and select "Guest Mode."

6. Toggle the slider to on or off.

How to connect to guest mode:

If you are the guest, you can cast your content to Google Home device without having to be connected to the Wi-Fi of the host. You do need to be connected to Wi-Fi to be able to connect through Guest mode. This could be your mobile data connection or a guest network.

1. Open whatever Chromecast-enabled app you want to use and select the cast button.

2. Choose "Nearby Device" and go through the steps that pop up.

3. If the pairing doesn't work, you will have to enter a 4-digit PIN that you will get from your host.

Where to Get the PIN

For a guest to connect with your Google Home, they will need a 4-digit PIN. When the guest tries to connect, your Google Home device will start to send the PIN to the phone using inaudible tones automatically. If the tone pairing doesn't work, the guest will be able to enter the PIN number to finish the pairing manually.

There are two places that the hose can find the PIN number.

Device Card:

1. Open your Google Home app.

2. Select the devices icon in the top right corner.

3. Locate the device that your guest is trying to locate to find it's PIN.

4. The PIN number is right below your device name.

Device Settings:

1. Open your Google Home app.

2. Select the devices icon in the top right corner.

3. Once you find the device card for the device you need, select the card menu and then select guest mode.

4. You will find the PIN number below "On." Give this number to the guest so that your guest can connect to your Google Home device.

Important:

Hosts and the guest that are using guest mode can turn on and turn off guest mode with any mobile device that has the Google Home app.

People who use guest mode can:

Cast content from their Android device with Android 4.3 or higher onto Google Home devices.

Cast content from their iOS device with iOS8 or higher. Bluetooth will have to be turned on to be able to cast content in guest mode.

This is an opt-in feature that the host can switch on or off from the app whenever you want to. Guest mode can be controlled from the app on an iOS or Android device.

If you perform a Factory Data Reset, your guest mode settings will be reset.

Other Methods of Playing Audio

Besides Android Audio, there are several other ways to listen to media on your Google Home.

Chromecast-Enabled Apps

You can easily play your favorite music on your Google Home device from Chromecast-enabled apps on your mobile devices. Your phone and tablet are also able to be used as a remote to help you control your Google Home playback.

Fist, cast your Chromecast-enabled apps to your Google Home device.

1. Your Google Home device, tablet, and phone all have to be connected to the same Wi-Fi network.

2. Open up your Chromecast-enabled app.

3. Select the cast icon.

4. Select Google Home device that you want to cast your app to.

5. Once the devices are connected, the icon will change colors showing you that everything is connected.

6. You are now able to cast audio to your Google Home device.

7. To turn off the cast, tap the icon again and then select "Stop Casting."

There are some providers that require you to have a subscription for you to play music from the app, such as YouTube Music and Spotify. If you are trying to cast from YouTube, you need to make sure you are in the YouTube Music app and not the regular YouTube app.

These voice commands will work with almost every single Chromecast-enabled app.

- To pause the music, say "Pause music" or "Pause."

- To resume the music, say "Continue playing" or "Resume."

- To stop the music, say "Stop music" or "Stop."

- To find out what is playing, say "What song is playing?" or "What's playing?"

Chrome Browser

There's no need to only listen to your music on your computer browser. You can listen to it from your Google Home as well. You can mirror the music that is playing on your computer to your Google Home device.

First, you have to begin by casting your Chrome browser.

1. Make sure you have the Chrome browser downloaded.

2. Make sure that your browser is up to date. If you start having problems, check to see if your browser is updated.

3. This isn't required, but it may help to pin the Cast button to your toolbar on Chrome.

4. Your Google Home device and your computer need to be connected to the same Wi-Fi.

You have several options to cast content from your browsers to your Google Home device. For all the options, your device and computer need to be on the same Wi-Fi network.

Cast Button:

1. Click the cast button on your browser. It should be in the top right corner of the browser.

2. Then select Google Home device that you want to connect to.

Chromecast-enabled Site:

1. Open the site that you want to connect, such as Google Play Music.

2. Select the cast button. This will normally be located where other controls are such as volume, pause, and play.

3. Select Google Home device that you want to connect to.

Chrome Menu:

1. Select the menu button in your Chrome browser, three vertical dots, in the upper right corner. Select "cast..." just below "print..."

2. Select Google Home device that you want to connect to.

Webpage:

1. Open up a Chrome browser tab.

2. Right-click the webpage and then select cast.

3. Select Google Home device that you want to connect to.

Most voice commands that you can use when listening to music aren't available when you are playing media from your browser. You can use volume commands, and the stop command.

News

You can listen to the news that you want to with your Google Home device. You can get information on certain categories, or you can find out about specific news information.

Here the voice commands that you can use to listen to the latest news:

- To hear the latest news, say: "Tell me the news" or "Catch me up."

- To hear news from a certain provider, say: "Listen to BBC Minute" or "Play NPR News."

- To hear the latest in a certain category, say: "What's the latest in [category]."

- To pause the news, say: "pause the news."

- To resume the news, say: "Continue playing."

- To stop the news, say: "Stop the news."

- To play the next story, say: "Skip."

- To find out what is currently playing, say: "What news is playing?"

It's helpful to know how to set up default news service on your Google Home device so that you can quickly access your favorite options.

1. Open up your Google Home app.

2. Tap the menu icon in the upper left-hand corner.

3. Make sure that the Google Account is showing the one you used when you setup your Google Home device. If it's not, use the triangle icon at the right of the name to change the accounts.

4. Once you have the correct account, select more settings and then news.

5. Here you will get a list of the news sources that may play whenever you say "Hey Google, listen to news."

6. To switch up the list order, press and hold the two horizontal marks that are next to the source. Drag the source where you want it on the list.

7. Here is how you can customize your list:

    a. Select customize.

b. To add in a new news source, select the check mark next to the sources that you are interested in having on your list.

c. To get rid of a news source, uncheck the check mark next to the sources that you don't want to have on your list.

This is the current list of the news categories that Google Home supports:

- Entertainment

- Art and Lifestyle

- Health

- Science

- Business

- Politics

- World

- Sports

- Technology

- General News

Radio

Along with the news, you can also listen to radio programs on your Google Home device. Here are the voice commands you can use to listen to radio broadcasts on your Google Home device and Chromecast-enabled speakers.

- To listen to a radio station that is in close range by name, say: "Play [station name]."

- To play a radio station by using its call-sign, say: "Play [call-sign]."

- To play a radio station by using its frequency, say: "Play [frequency]."

- To play a radio station in another state by its frequency, say: "Play [frequency] [state]."

- To listen to a radio station on a Chromecast-enabled speaker or TV, say: "Play [station name] on [device name]"

- To listen to a nearby NPR station, say: "Play NPR."

- To pause the radio, say: "Pause the radio."

- To resume the radio, say: "Resume."

- To stop the radio, say: "Stop the radio."

- To find out what is playing, say: "What's playing?"

If you have problems playing a radio station, here are some troubleshooting options:

1. If it doesn't want to play a station that you asked for, try being more specific with your

request, or try to ask for a station in a different way, such as call sign, frequency, or name.

2. If Google Home doesn't return with what you requested, then try adding "on TuneIn." For example, "Play BBC Radio on TuneIn."

3. When you ask for a station by frequency, but you don't get the right station, try adding in a city that's nearby, such as "Play 101.9 FM LA".

Music

You can use Google Home to listen to music from many different services by asking for activity, mood, playlist, album, genre, song, or artist. At this time, Google Home only supports one account per service.

Here are the basic commands to play music on your Google Home through all service providers.

- To request a certain song, say: "Play [song]", "Play [song] by [artist]", or "Play [song] on [service]".

- To request a certain artist, say: "Play [artist]", or "Play [artist] on [service]".

- To request a certain album, say: "Play [album]", "Play [album] by [artist]", or "Play [album] by [artist] on [service]".

- To listen to music based on activity, mood, or genre, say: "Play [genre] on [service]," "Play music for exercising," "Play love music," or "Play rock music."

- To listen to personalized music from a certain service, say: "Play [genre] music on [service]," or "Play some music."

- To listen to music on a video device, TV, or speakers (your device has to be linked), say: "Play [genre] on bedroom speakers" or "Play music on living room TV."

- To pause music, say: "Pause the music."

- To resume music, say: "Continue playing."

- To stop the music, say: "Stop music."

- To listen to the next song, say: "Next song."

- To find out what is playing, say: "What song is playing?"

Here are some commands to use for subscription and free music services:

Google Play Music:

You will have to purchase a premium subscription to listen to certain songs, artists, and albums. If you don't use a premium service, you will only get to listen to a music station made up of songs that were inspired by artists, albums, and songs that you chose.

The Google Account that was used when Google Home device was set up will be the default

account for Google Play Music. You cannot
change this.

- To play a playlist in your library, say: "Play
  [playlist]."

- To listen to a certain album, say: "Play
  [album]."

- To listen to the last song, say "Previous."

- To skip forward to a song, say: "Skip
  forward [time]."

- To shuffle your playlist, say: "Shuffle."

- To listen to a song again, say: "Repeat the
  song" or "Play it again."

- To loop a playlist, say: "Repeat [on or off]."

At the moment, you are not able to directly play
purchased or uploaded Google Play Music
content. You can, however, put the purchased

content into a playlist and play it with the command "Hey Google, play [name] playlist."

Pandora:

If you have used Pandora before, you know that you're not able to request a specific artist, album, or song. You only get a mixture of songs based on artist, album, or songs that you select.

You will first need to link your Pandora account with your Google Home.

Here are basic commands you can use with your Google Home to listen to your Pandora account:

- To listen to a personalized radio station on Pandora, say "Play my shuffle."

- To listen to a radio station based on songs you've thumbed up on Pandora, say: "Play my Thumbprint radio."

- To play a certain playlist, say: "Play [Pandora station]."

- To like or dislike a song, say: "I like this song," "Thumbs down," or "Thumbs up."

YouTube Music:

To use YouTube, you will have to have a YouTube Red subscription to listen to request specific artists, albums, and songs. You will need a subscription for most of the functionality.

Make sure that the Google account you used to setup your Google Home is the same Google account you use for your YouTube account.

Here are some basic commands to use with your YouTube music account:

- To like or dislike a song, say: "Thumbs [up or down]."

- To like or dislike a station, say: "[Follow or Unfollow] this station."

- To listen to the last song, say "Previous."

- To skip forward a certain amount a time, say: "Skip forward [time]."

- To listen to a song again, say: "Play song again."

At the moment, if you say "Hey Google, stop casting" when listening to YouTube Music, it only pauses the music. To stop the music, you will have to do it manually in the Google Home app.

Spotify:

You have to have a premium account to listen to Spotify on your Google Home.

Here are some basic commands to use with your Spotify account:

- To play the songs in your Spotify library, say: "Play my library."

- To play a certain playlist, say: "Play [playlist name]."

- To like or dislike a song, say: "I [like or dislike] this song."

- To like or dislike a station, say: "[Save or Unsave] this station."

- To listen to the last song, say "Previous."

- To skip the song forward a little while, say: "Skip forward [time]."

- To shuffle a playlist, say: "Shuffle."

- To put a playlist on loop, say: "Repeat [on or off]"

At the moment, you aren't able to listen to podcasts on Spotify with Google Home.

Here is how you can connect your music and set up your default music service. This is the service that will be used first when you ask for music to be played.

1. Open up your Google Home app.

2. Select the menu icon and then select music.

3. To select a default, select the radio icon at the left side of the music service.

4. To link a functionality:

    a. With a YouTube Red or Google Play Music, your account will be automatically linked once you set up your Google Home.

    b. You will have to link your Pandora and Spotify accounts.

        i. Select link to begin the connection

        ii. You will then have to sign in or sign up for an account

        iii. If you want to unlink, just select unlink

Music services:

1. Pandora

2. Spotify

3. YouTube Music

4. Google Play Music

How to Link TVs and Speakers

You can use you Google Home device with your TVs and speakers that have Chromecast built-in, Chromecast Audio plugged in, or Chromecast.

First, you will need to link your TVs and speakers.

Link with Google Home:

1.   Set up your Google Home device.

2.   Open up your Google Home app.

3.   Select the menu icon in the upper left corner.

4.   Make sure that you are logged in to the correct Google Account.

5.   Make sure that all the devices are connected to the same Wi-Fi network.

6. Select "More Settings" and the "TVs and Speakers." You will then see a list of all the devices that you have linked.

7. To link any new TVs or speakers that have Chromecast built-in select the plus symbol at the bottom right.

8. The app with then starts to search for the voice-supported TV or speaker with the same Wi-Fi network that your Google Home is connected to. You may end up seeing a list of devices that aren't voice-supported. At the moment, you aren't able to link these devices.

9. Tap the box next to the name of the device to connect it. You can select several devices at one, and then select add.

10. These will now show up in the TVs and speakers section of the app.

11. If you receive and error message, you will need to perform a Factory Data Reset on your Chromecast device.

To make sure you receive proper playback with your TVs or speakers, use the next tips to name the devices:

1. Name each of your Chromecast Audio, built-in, and Google Home devices with a different name.

    a. A good example would be:

        i. Google Home: Rec room

        ii. Chromecast device: Family speaker

    b. A bad example would be:

        i. Google Home: Family Room Home

        ii. Chromecast device: Family Room Speaker

2. It helps to make sure that the name of your device is pronounceable.

3. Make sure you don't use any special characters or emoji.

This is how you can change the name of your devices:

1. Open up your Google Home app.

2. Select the devices icon so that you can see all the connected devices.

3. Scroll until you locate the device that you want to change the name of.

4. In the device, card selects the menu icon and select name.

5. Delete whatever its current name is and then tap in the new name. Select save.

These are the current devices that you can connect with your Google Home:

1. Android TV devices. At the moment, you aren't able to connect Spotify to Android TV devices.

2. Speakers and TVs that have Chromecast built-in. Android TVs and speakers and TVs with built-in Chromecast need to have a cast version of 1.21 or higher.

3. Chromecast Audio

4. Chromecast

Here are some of the basic commands that you can use to control your TVs or speakers with Google Home:

- To play your music on a certain device by name, say: "Play [artist] using [Pandora] on [device name]."

- You can use any music control commands just add the device name to the command.

- You can't play news or podcasts at the present moment

Movies and TV Shows

At the moment, you are only able to use Netflix with Google Home. If you have a premium YouTube subscription, you can play TV shows and videos on Google Home.

Once you have linked your TV, you can move onto linking your video apps.

1. Open up your Google Home app.

2. Select the menu icon in the upper left corner.

3. Make sure that you are logged into the correct Google Account before you continue.

4. Make sure that everything is setup and that they are all connected to the same Wi-Fi network.

5. Select "More Settings" and the "Videos and photos."

6. In the video section, scroll until you locate the video app that you want.

7. If the app needs to be linked, select "link" and then "link account." Google Home will automatically connect your Netflix profile. Secondary profiles are not allowed or supported.

8. Continue to the sign in.

Now you can control your movies and TV shows with Google Home.

- To play movie, show, or series, say: "Watch [show name] on Netflix [TV name].

  o When you request a TV series, it will pick up from where you last session ended. Requesting a certain episode isn't currently supported.

- To watch the next or last episode, say: "Previous episode [show name]" or "Next episode [show name]."

- To stop, resume, or pause, say: "Stop [TV name]", "Resume [TV name] or Pause [TV name].

- To move to a specific area in a show, say: "Skip back [time] [TV name]"

- To turn subtitles off or on, say: "Turn on subtitles" or "Turn off subtitles."

Multi Playback

With Google Home, you can combine any Chromecast built-in speakers, Chromecast Audio devices, or Google Home devices together for the same music to play throughout your house. All your favorite audio and music from Chromecast apps are available to stream.

At the moment, you aren't able to sync multi-room video devices.

The first step is to create your audio groups.

1. Open up the Google Home app.

2. Select the devices icon in the top right-hand corner to find all the audio devices that you have available. Keep in mind everything must be connected to the same Wi-Fi network.

3. Select the menu icon in the upper right-hand corner of the device that you want to group. Then select "Create Group."

4. The group will automatically be named Homegroup. You can rename the group by erasing the name and then type in whatever you want your group to be named.

5. After that, a list of available devices will be shown.

6. Tap the box that is next to the device name to add or remove that device from your group. If there is a blue check mark in the box, you know that device is part of your group. You have to have at least two devices selected to create a group. Select save.

7. After you have successfully created your group, your group will now have a card under the devices tab. Know that it can

take up to ten seconds for your new group to show up in your Google Home app. Select "Speakers in Group" to find out all the devices that are in your group.

8. On your group card, you will find a ribbon that says "Enable voice control and more." Select this to confirm your group link. You can also link the group in the Assistant settings, which is located under "TV and Speakers."

9. To make sure that the group is voice-enabled and linked, select the overflow menu on your group card and select "Linked Accounts."

To enable voice control:

1. Select the devices icon in the upper right-hand corner.

2. Scroll until finding the group card that you need.

3. Select the banner, which is blue that reads "Enabled voice control and more" then select "Yes I'm In."

To edit a group:

1. Open up your Google Home app.

2. Select the devices icon in the upper right corner.

3. Scroll until you find the group card that you need to edit.

4. Select the device in the menu in the upper right corner of the group card, and then select "Edit Group." This will give you a list of all the speakers that are in your group.

5. Select the box next to the devices that you want to add or remove from your group. The speakers that you already have in your group will have a blue checkmark next to it.

6. Select save once you have finished editing your group.

7. After all the changes to the group have been saving, a message will appear at the bottom of the screen that will confirm that the changes have been made.

8. If you are trying to make changes to a group that is casting music, your playback will stop, and you won't be able to listen to the music on any of the speakers that are in that group. After you are finished editing, you will have to go back to the app to begin casting music again.

Delete a group:

1. Open up your Google Home app.

2. Select the Device icon in the top right-hand corner.

3. Scroll until you find the group card that you want.

4. Select the group menu in the top right corner of the group card. Then select "Delete Group" and then "Delete."

5. If you delete a group that is casting music, your playback will immediately stop, and you won't be able to listen to music on the connected devices in that group.

6. After you have deleted the group, you will receive a message confirming that you have deleted the group. Also, you will no longer see a group card under the devices tab.

Once you have the group set up and everything linked, you are ready to control your group by voice. When you communicate with the group, it is just like talking to a single device. The main difference is that you will say [group name] instead of [device name]. You need to make sure that voice-enabled is turned on for the group.

Here are some commands to use with your new group.

- To have device group play music, say: "Play classical on [group]."

- To control the playback with basic commands, say: "[stop, resume, pause, skip] song on [group name]."

- To control the volume, say: "Set volume to 50%". When you a listening to music on a group, when you use a volume command, it will only change the sound on your Google Home device unless you make sure you say "Hey Google ... on [group name].

Photos

With your Google Home, and your Chromecast, voice-supported, TV, you can view a slideshow of all your pictures in your Google Photos library. To do so, you have to a Chromecast or a TV that has Chromecast built-in that is linked to your Google Home.

The first step is to set up your TV to display your photos.

Link TV:

1. Open up your Google Home app.

2. Select the menu icon in the upper left-hand corner.

3. Make sure that you are logged into the correct Google Account. If not, switch accounts using the triangle at the right of the name showing.

4. Make sure that all the devices are connected to the same Wi-Fi network.

5. Select "More Settings" then "TVs and Speakers." This will show you a list of your linked devices.

6. To link a new TV, select the plus icon located at the lower right corner.

7. Your app will then begin to search for all the voice-supported TVs that are currently linked to the same Wi-Fi network. It may pull up a list of TVs that aren't voice-supported. You can't link those TVs with your Google Home.

8. Select the checkbox next to the devices that you want to link to your Google Home. Then select add.

9. These new devices will show up in the TVs and speakers section of the app.

10. While linking, if you get an "Error when linking device" you will have to perform a Factory Data Reset on the Chromecast device.

Personal Results:

1. Open up your Google Home app.

2. Select the menu icon in the upper left corner.

3. Make sure that you are logged in to the correct Google Account. If not, switch accounts by tapping the triangle icon to the right.

4. Select "More Settings."

5. Scroll until you find "Adjust settings for this Google Home device."

6. Select Google Home device from the down arrow list that you are interested in configuring. If you only own and have

linked, one Google Home, you won't receive the down arrow.

7. In the "Personal results" section, switch the slider to the on position.

Allow Google Photos:

1. Open your Google Home app.

2. Select the menu icon in the upper left corner.

3. Makes sure that you are logged into the correct Google account. If not, switch accounts by selecting the triangle icon to the right.

4. Select "More Settings" and then select "Videos and photos."

5. Once in the photo section, switch the slider to on.

The photos that will show are the ones that are associated with the account that you used to set up your Google Home device.

Now you can view your photo on your linked TVs with these commands.

- To see photos of a certain person (face grouping), say: "Show me photos of [name] on [device]." Face grouping is only available in certain countries.

- To see photos of a certain place, say: "Show me photos of [place] on [device]."

- To see photos from a certain date, say: "Show me photos from [date] on [device]."

- To see photos from a certain album, say: "Show me photos from [album] on [device]."

You can only use the commands for photos that you have backed-up in your Google Photos account.

After you have used one of the commands from above to begin the slideshow, the Google Photo logo will show up on your TV once the slideshow has opened. After the slideshow, has appeared you can use these commands to control your photo slideshow.

When you say one of the following commands, you will get a confirmation in the upper left corner of the screen.

- To move to the next photo, say: "Next slide on [device]."

- To move to the previous photo, say: "the Previous slide on [device]."

- To pause your slideshow, say: "Pause photos on [device]."

- To resume your slideshow, say: "Resume slideshow on [device]."

- To stop your slideshow, say: "Stop slideshow on [device]."

Your slideshow will show your most recent pictures at the beginning. It will remove lower quality and duplicate pictures.

To keep from having your photos display on a TV:

If you have your personal results turned on, your photos will display on any TV that is connected to your Google Home device by default. Follow these steps to turn off this feature.

1. Open your Google Home app.

2. Select the menu icon in the upper left corner.

3. Makes sure you logged in with the correct Google account. If now, switch the account by pressing the triangle icon to the right of the name.

4. Select "More Settings" and the select "Videos and photos."

5. Once in the photo section, switch the slider to off.

Be in Control of Your Home

With your Google Home, you can control your smart home apps with just your voice. Google Home, now, only works with things controlled by SmartThings, Philips Hue, Nest, Honeywell, and Belkin Wemo.

Connect SmartThings

To be able to control your SmartThings devices, you first have to connect them with your Google Home.

1. Begin by downloading the app for SmartThings and created an account,

2. Your Google Assistant will require that you use either Google Pixel or Google Home to connect with SmartThings,

    a. With Google Home, you will need you have the Google Home app

before you can connect your
SmartThings devices.

b. If you're using Google Pixel, you will
    connect directly through Google
    Assistant.

Connecting your Google Assistant with your
SmartThings devices:

1. Open your Google Home app.

2. Tap the menu icon in the top left corner.

3. Make sure that you are logged in to the
    correct Google Account. If not, switch by
    tapping the triangle to the right of the
    name.

4. Select "Home control."

5. Select the Devices icon and then select the
    plus button at the bottom right.

6. Select SmartThings.

7. Log into your SmartThings account.

8. Select the "Log in" button.

9. Select your SmartThings location from the "From" menu.

10. Select all the devices that you want to connect with your Google Assistant. It's best that you only select lights and thermostats, and don't select cameras, sirens, or garage door openers.

11. Select authorize.

12. You can then assign the device to certain rooms or your and select "Done" and then "Got it."

You have the ability to assign your SmartThings devices to certain rooms. When you do assign your devices to certain rooms, you can control several lights as a group. First, you will have to add rooms in Google Home Control, and then you will assign the devices to certain rooms.

Rooms in Google Home Control are different that the rooms you have in your SmartThings app. Your Google Assistant won't recognize and of your SmartThings Rooms. You will have to assign your devices to certain rooms in your Google Home Control for your Google Assistant to recognize them.

1. Open your Google Home app.

2. Select the menu icon in the upper left corner.

3. Select "Home Control."

4. Select "Rooms."

5. Select the plus button located at the bottom right.

6. Choose the room that you want to add. If you don't see a room that you want to add, you can select "Custom Room."

7. Select "Done."

8. Select the "Devices" tab.

9. Choose the device that you want to assign to a specific room.

10. Select "Room."

11. Then select which room that you want to assign you device to.

12. Select the back arrow, and do this again to make more rooms, and to add more devices to rooms.

Once you have connected your Google Assistant to your SmartThings devices, you can still add new devices when you get them. Follow these steps to do so.

1. Open your Google Home app.

2. Select the menu icon at the upper left corner.

3. Select "Home control."

4. Select the vertical dots in the right corner.

5. Select "Manage Accounts."

6. Select "SmartThings."

7. Select "Check for new devices."

8. Select the location of your device in the "From" menu.

9. Select "Authorize."

10. You will see the new devices listed on your screen.

Controlling Your Lights

With your Google Home, you can control your lights if you have Philips Hue or SmartThings lights. Google Home doesn't support Philips Hue Scenes.

Before you begin, make sure that you:

*   Have setup your Google Home.

- Your tablet or phone is connected to the correct Wi-Fi network

- Make sure the Google account you are logged in with, is the one that you setup your Google Home with.

- Have SmartThings connected lights or Philips Hue lights.

Begin by setting up your lights.

Each provider should give you instructions to set up your lights, so make sure you do that before you try to connect them to your Google Home.

Philips Hue:

1. Create an account with Hue if haven't done so already.

2. Follow their steps to set up the lights.

3. Make sure that your Google Home and Hue bridge are connected to the same Wi-Fi network.

SmartThings:

1. Follow their steps to set up your lights correctly.

Next, you need to connect your lights with your Google Home.

1. Open up your Google Home app.

2. Select the menu icon at the upper left corner.

3. Select "Home control."

4. In your devices tab, you will have a list of the all the lights that you have to connect with your Google Home

5. To add new lights, select the plus symbol at the bottom right of the screen.

6. Select the light provider that you are using to link your lights.

7. Philips Hue:

a. Select "Philips Hue" and then select "Pair."

b. Select the link button located on your Philips Hue bridge.

c. Select "Assign Rooms."

d. After the pairing has finished, you will be able to assign your lights to your rooms, or select "Done."

8. SmartThings:

a. Select "SmartThings."

b. Log into your SmartThings account.

c. Read over the info that will be used when you connect your lights to your Google Home.

d. Choose the lights that you want to connect to your Google Home.

e. Select "Authorize."

f. Now assign your lights to certain rooms if you would like.

There are no limits to how many devices that you link to your Google Home.

Next, you can rename or select a nickname for your lights.

You can name a light with the same name that it has in the SmartThings or Philips Hue app, or you can give it a nickname within your Google Home app.

1. In the devices tab, you will have a list of lights that are connected to your Google Home.

2. Select the light that you want to give a nickname.

3. Select "Set a nickname."

4. Put in your nickname for the device and then select "ok" and then "device details."

5. You will now see the light with its nickname that you just gave it.

These nicknames won't be shown in the SmartThings or Philips Hue app.

Next, you can assign lights to certain rooms.

Add Room:

1. In the "Rooms" tab, there will be a list of lights that are connected to your Google Home.

2. Tap the plus sign to add a light.

3. To select a room, select the radio button at the left of the name then select next.

   a. If the room want isn't listed, scroll and select "Custom Room."

   b. Add the name of the room and then select ok.

4. You will then get a list of lights that are linked. Select the box next to the light that you want to add to a room. Then select done.

Add Lights:

1. In the "Rooms" tab, there will be a list of your rooms and then lights that are assigned to them.

2. Select the room that you want to adjust.

3. There will be a list of the lights that are already assigned to the room, and lights listed under "Add devices."

4. Under "Add devices" select the box next to the lights that you want to add to the room, or choose "Select all" if you want to add all of them.

5. Select "Done."

6. Then you will receive an updated light list for that room.

Check for lights:

1. Philips Hue

   a. Under the Devices tab, you will get a list of "Unassigned" devices.

   b. Go through the steps for a nickname for the device and then add them to a room.

2. SmartThings

   a. Under the devices tab, there will be a list of "Unassigned" devices.

   b. Select "More" and then "Manage Accounts."

   c. Select the account where you want to check for new lights.

   d. Select "Check for new devices" then select the location in the list, and then select "Authorize."

e. You see some lights you added at the bottom of the screen.

f. Follow the steps from above to add the lights to a room.

Change Room:

1. In the rooms tab, there will be a list of rooms and the lights assigned to them.

2. Select the room that you want to adjust.

3. Select the light that you want to move and select the "Move" button.

4. Select the radio button located next to the room name that you want to move the light to.

    a. You can add an extra room by pressing "Custom Room."

5. Select done.

6. The light will no longer be listed in the original room.

Rename Room:

1. In the rooms tab, there will be a list of rooms and the lights that are assigned to them.

2. Select the room that you want to change.

3. Choose the room's name.

4. Write in the new name. Select "ok" and then "done."

5. The lights will now be listed under the room with the new name.

Delete Room:

1. First, you need to take out any devices that are assigned to that room.

2. In the rooms tab, there will be a list of rooms and the lights that are assigned to them.

3. Select the room that you want to delete.

4. Select the trash can that is located at the top of the screen

5. Select "ok" to confirm your decision.

Now you're ready to control your lights with your voice. Here are some basic commands that you can use.

- To turn your lights on or off, say: "Turn off [name]."

- To dim your lights, say: "Dim the [name]."

- To brighten your lights, say: "Brighten the [name]."

- To set the brightness to a percentage, say: "Set [name] to 80%".

- To brighten or dim a light by a percentage, say: "[Brighten or dim] [name] by 60%".

- To switch the light color, say: "Turn [name] red."

- To turn the lights in a room on or off, say: "Turn [on or off] lights in [room],"

- To turn all the lights off or on, say: "Turn [on or off] all of the lights."

If you want to unlink any of your lights, there are two ways to do so.

Google Home app:

1. In the Devices tab, there will be a list or rooms and the lights assigned to them.

2. Select the more icon in the top right and then select "manage accounts."

3. Select the account that you want to unlink.

4. Select "Unlink account" and then "unlink."

5. A confirmation will pop up on the screen.

SmartThings or Philips Hue app:

1. If you choose to unlink a light from the partner app and not the Google Home app, it's best also to unlink the lights within the Google Home app.

Control Thermostats

Now let's look at how you can control your thermostats with your voice if you have a thermostat connected to SmartThings, Honeywell Thermostat, or a Nest Thermostat.

Before you begin, make sure that you:

- Have setup your Google Home.

- Your tablet or phone is connected to the correct Wi-Fi network

- Make sure the Google account you are logged in with, is the one that you setup your Google Home with.

- Make sure you have a Nest or Honeywell thermostat, or a thermostat that is connected with SmartThings.

  - Google Home doesn't support lyric thermostats, only total connect comfort thermostats.

First, you need to make sure that you have your thermostat set up the way that the manufacturer states.

Next, you need to connect your lights with your Google Home.

1. Open up your Google Home app.

2. Select the menu icon at the upper left corner.

3. Select "Home control."

4. In your devices tab, you will have a list of the all the thermostats that you have to connect with your Google Home

5. To add new thermostats, select the plus symbol at the bottom right of the screen.

6. Select the thermostat provider that you are using to link your thermostats.

7. Nest:

    a. Select Nest.

    b. Make sure to check the info that will be shared when you link your Nest thermostat with Google Home.

    c. If you have never connected a Nest thermostat, you will need to log into your Nest account. Then select continue.

    d. If there is more than on home in your account, then make sure that you pick the home that you want to connect to your Google Home.

8. SmartThings:

   a. Select SmartThings.

   b. Log into your account.

   c. Read over the information that will be used when connecting

   d. Choose the thermostats that you want to connect.

   e. Select Authorize.

9. Honeywell:

   a. Select Honeywell.

   b. Select your device.

   c. Log into you Honeywell account.

   d. Read everything this is going to use when you connect the two.

You can rename your thermostats in the exact same manner as you can your lights. Follow the steps above if you wish to do so.

Add Room:

1. In the "Rooms" tab, there will be a list of thermostats and the rooms they are assigned to.

2. Tap the plus sign.

3. To select a room, select the radio button at the left of the name then select next.

    a. If the room want isn't listed, scroll and select "Custom Room."

    b. Add the name of the room and then select ok.

4. You will then get a list of thermostats that are linked. Select the box next to the thermostat that you want to add to a room. Then select done.

Add Thermostats:

1. In the "Rooms" tab, there will be a list of your rooms and the thermostats that are assigned to them.

2. Select the room that you want to adjust.

3. There will be a list of the thermostats that are already assigned to the room, and thermostats listed under "Add devices."

4. Under "Add devices" select the box next to the thermostats that you want to add to the room, or choose "Select all" if you want to add all of them.

5. Select "Done."

6. Then you will receive an updated thermostats list for that room.

Check for Thermostats:

SmartThings

1. Under the devices tab, there will be a list of rooms and the thermostats assigned to them.

2. Select "More" and then "Manage Accounts."

3. Select the account where you want to check for new thermostats.

4. Select "Check for new devices" then select the location in the list, and then select "Authorize."

5. You see some thermostats you added at the bottom of the screen.

6. Follow the steps from above to add the thermostat to a room.

Change Room:

1. In the rooms tab, there will be a list of rooms and the thermostats assigned to them.

2. Select the room that you want to adjust.

3. Select the thermostat that you want to move and select the "Move" button.

4. Select the radio button located next to the room name that you want to move the light to.

   a. You can add an extra room by pressing "Custom Room."

5. Select done.

6. The thermostat will no longer be listed in the original room.

Deleting and renaming thermostats work the same way that it does for lights. Please follow the above directions to do so.

For Nest only, when you change the name of a device in your Google Home app, the name won't change in the Nest app. If you change the name of the device in the Nest app, it will update the name of the thermostat in your Google Home app.

Now you are ready to control your thermostats by voice. Here are some basic commands to control your thermostats.

- To change the temperature, say: "Set temperature to 72" or "Make it [warmer or cooler]."

- To switch from cooling or heating modes, say: "Set thermostat to [cooling or heating]."

- To set the temperature, say: "Set heat to 72" or "Set air conditioning to 75".

- To turn your thermostat off, say: "Turn off thermostat."

- To change the temperature using the room name, say: "Set the [room] thermostat to 75".

- To find out what the temperature is in the room, say: "What's the temperature inside?"

- To find out what you have the temperature is set to, say: "What's the thermostat set to?"

You can unlink your thermostats in the same what that you unlink lights. If you need to unlink one, follow the steps above.

Switches or Plugs

If you have switches or plugs connected to SmartThings, or if you have Belkin Wemo switches or plugs, you can control them with your voice through your Google Home.

Before you begin, make sure that you:

- Have setup your Google Home.

- Your tablet or phone is connected to the correct Wi-Fi network

- Make sure the Google account you are logged in with, is the one that you setup your Google Home with.

- Make sure that you have a Belking Wemo switch or plug, or s switch or plug connected with SmartThings.

First, you need to make sure that you have you switches or plugs set up the way that the manufacturer states.

Next, you need to connect your lights with your Google Home.

1. Open up your Google Home app.

2. Select the menu icon at the upper left corner.

3. Select "Home control."

4. In your devices tab, you will have a list of the all the switches or plugs that you have to connect with your Google Home

5. To add new switches or plugs, select the plus symbol at the bottom right of the screen.

6. Select the thermostat provider that you are using to link your thermostats.

7. SmartThings:

   a. Select SmartThings.

   b. Log into your account.

   c. Read over the information that will be used when connecting

   d. Choose the switches or plugs that you want to connect.

   e. Select Authorize.

8. Belkin Wemo:

a. Select Wemo and then "Ready to Verify."

b. At the switch or plug, switch the power off and then back on. You only have two minutes to do this.

c. Select "Yes, that's me." There may be a bit of a lag before you see the prompt.

You can rename your thermostats in the exact same manner as you can your lights. Follow the steps above if you wish to do so.

Adding rooms and thermostats work the same as the above directions. You can only add a switch or plug to one room. You can't assign one switch or plug to multiple rooms.

Check for Switch or Plugs:

1. Under the devices tab, there will be a list of rooms and the switches or plugs assigned to them.

2. Select "More" and then "Manage Accounts."

3. Select the account where you want to check for new switches or plugs.

4. Select "Check for new devices" then select the location in the list, and then select "Authorize."

5. You see a number of switches and plugs you added at the bottom of the screen.

6. Follow the steps from above to add them to a room.

You can switch the rooms that the switches and plugs are in the same way that you can switch the rooms for lights and thermostats, so follow the directions above.

Deleting and renaming thermostats work the same way that it does for lights. Please follow the above directions to do so.

Now you are ready to use voice commands to control your switches and plugs. Here are some basic commands to use

- To turn a plug on or off, say: "Turn [on or off] the [name].

- To turn a switch on or off, say: "Turn [on or off] the [name].

If you need to unlink a switch or plug you can follow the same steps that are listed above for lights.

Lists, Alarms, and Timers

With your Google Home, you can set and control timers, alarms, and lists with just the sound of your voice.

Alarms

Here are commands to use to manage and set alarms:

- To create a new alarm, say: "Set alarm for [time]."

- To create an alarm with a name, say: "Set alarm for [time] called [name]."

- To create a repeating alarm, say: "Set alarm for [time] every day of the week."

- To ask about an alarm, say: "When is my alarm?"

- To cancel and alarm, say: "Cancel my alarm."

- To turn off a ringing alarm, say: "Stop."

- To snooze, say: "Snooze."

Here are some commands to control your alarm volume:

- To turn up the volume, say "Louder."

- To turn the volume down, say: "Softer."

- To set it to a specific volume, say: "Volume level six."

- To set to max volume, say: "Max volume."

- To set to a minimum volume, say: "Minimum volume".

- To adjust the volume by a certain amount, say: "[increase or decrease] by 30%".

- To find out the volume level, say: "What's the volume?"

Timers

You can easily set a timer for laundry, cooking, or other activities using your Google Home. Here are some basic commands.

- To set a timer with and without a name, say: "Set timer for [time]" or "Set a [time] timer for [name]."

- To find out how much time is left, say: "How much time is left?"

- To cancel a timer, say: "Cancel timer."

- To turn off a timer, say: "Stop."

- To pause a timer, say: "Pause timer."

- To resume a timer, say: "Resume timer."

Lists

You can also use your Google Home to create a shopping list and other types of lists. Here are some basic commands to use.

- To add an item to a list, say: "Add [item] to my shopping list."

- To check what is on your list, say: "What's on my shopping list."

Information and More

With Google Home, you can begin your day by hearing the information that you need to start your day correctly.

First, you need to set up your day.

1. In the Google Home app, select the menu icon.

2. Select "more settings" and the select "my day."

3. Select the options that you want to have included in your "My Day" summary:

   a. Weather

   b. Commute

   c. Meetings

   d. Reminders

4. Then choose how you want your summary to be ended:

   a. If you want it to end with the news, select the button next to news

   b. If you don't want it to end with anything, select the button next to nothing.

5. Make sure you turn on personal results.

In the morning, all you have to do to hear you're my day summary is, say "Hey Google, tell me about My Day."

The things you can add to your summary are:

Weather – what the forecast for the day looks like.

Commute – you will hear what the traffic will be like for your travel to work, and how long it should take.

Reminder – you will hear all the reminders you have set for yourself for the day.

Calendar – this is will tell you about any meetings you have for the day. Your calendar has to be connected with the same Google Account.

Flight Status – this will tell you about the status of a flight that you are planning. This option can't be turned off.

Commute and Traffic

When you want to find out what traffic is like, all you have to do is ask your Google Home. You can find out estimated travel time, traffic condition, and commute.

First, you need to manage your commute information. You need to set your home and work locations and well as the address of your Google Home device.

Here are some basic commands to use when you need to find out about traffic:

- To find out commute conditions, say: "How long is my commute?"

- To specify a method, say: "How long will it take to [method] to the [location]?"

- To a specific destination, say: "How long will it take to get to [location]?"

- To get to a specific destination from a specific source, say: "How long will it take to get from [location] to [destination]?"

Forecast and Weather

You can find out current weather conditions and upcoming weather by asking your Google Home. First, you will have to set up the address for your Google Home and set your preferred unit.

Here are some commands you can use when asking about the weather:

- To find out the current weather, say: "What's the weather?"

- To ask for a forecast, say: "What's the weather for [amount of time, weekend, day, or tomorrow]?"

- To find out specific information about the weather, say: "Is it going to be sunny tomorrow?", "Do I need an umbrella?", or "Is is going to snow today?"

- To find out about the weather in a specific location, say: "What's the weather for [day] in [location]?"

- To find out a general weather question in a location, say: "What's the weather in [location]?"

- To specify a certain unit, say: "What's the weather in Fahrenheit?"

Business

You can use your Google Home to find out information about places around town.

Here are some basic commands to use for certain business information:

- To find out where nearby locations are, say: "Where are [business] nearby?", "Any [business] nearby?", or "Find me a restaurant."

- To get the phone number for a business, say: "What is a [business] phone number?"

- To get the address of a business, say: "What is [business] address?"

- To get the hours of operation for a business, say: "Is [business] in [location] open now?"

Make sure you are as specific as possible with your question. This will make sure you get the best answer possible.

Event and Calendar

You can ask your Google Home device about the events you have on your calendar. You aren't able to add calendar events using voice control. Google Home only supports events that are in your main calendar that is associated with your Google Account that was used to setup your device.

Unsupported Calendars:

- Calendar subscriptions – any calendars that you are subscribed to.

- Shared calendars – any calendars that you share with other users.

- Other calendars – these are any other calendars that don't fall into the other categories or are associated with a Google Account that wasn't used to set up your Google Home.

Here are some basic commands that you can use
to get event and calendar information:

- To get information on one event or meeting
  that's coming up, say: "[Where, when, or
  what] is my first [event or meeting]?"

- To get information about multiple events,
  say: "List my events for [date]."

Flight Information

You can use your Google Home to find out
information about any upcoming flights that you
have.

Here are some basic commands to use to get flight
information:

- To get the origin, destination, airline, time,
  or day for an upcoming flight, say: "My
  next flight," "When is my upcoming
  flight?", or "My flight to [destination]."

- To find out the time or delay status, say: "Is my flight on time?" "Is my flight delayed?"

- To hear any information for multiple upcoming flights (this will give you information for the next three flights), say: "What times are my flights?" or "My flights in [month]."

Manage and Set Up Services

You can use your Google Home with other third-party services and add an extra performance layer.

First, browse all the available services.

1. In the app select the menu icon.

2. Select "More Settings" and the "services."

3. Scroll through the different services and select whatever services look good to you.

4. You can read about the service and see a list of the things that it can do.

Then you can link or unlink the service.

Link:

1. In the services tab, select the card that you are interested in linking.

2. Select "Link service."

3. Log into the service if needed. This step changes depending on the services.

Unlink:

1. In the services tab, select the card that you are interested in unlinking.

2. Select "unlink" and then "unlink" to confirm that you do want to unlink the service.

Here are some basic commands you can use to communicate with these services.

- To begin a service, say: "Let me talk to [name]," "At [name]," or "Speak to [name]."

Privacy

A common concern with Google Home is how safe your privacy is using it. With the fact that it is always on, this is a very common concern among users.

Google Home does not record all your conversations. Google Home only listens in for a few second snippets for keywords. The snippets are then deleted if Google Home doesn't hear one of the keywords, and no information leaves your device on it hears a keyword. When your device hears "Hey Google" or "Ok Google" the light on top will turn on letting you know that it is recording. The system sends the recording to Google to fulfill your request based on the keywords that it recognizes.

Another common concern is if people can hear your conversation, search, or location history. If a person is near your device, they can request information from your Google Home. If you gave your device access to your personal information, Gmail, or calendars, then anybody that is near your device can ask for this information. Google Home also picks up information about you from the way you interact with your other Google services.

You may also be wondering if your Google Home shares your information with other companies, advertisers, apps, Google, contacts, or anyone. Google doesn't sell any of your personal information to anybody. They do sometimes share your information with third parties under certain circumstances. When you use your Google Home for something like Uber, it will send the information necessary to the app to complete your requested action. With this, you will already have given Google permission to do so.

Support

When you get a new device, there are some things that may come up that you need help with. This chapter will cover some helpful information that may help you to troubleshoot some problems.

Of course, you can contact a Google Home expert whenever you need help. There are several different locations that you can use to get helpful information. This is just for Google Home and does not apply to any other Google product.

You can get information from the Google Home help forum. There you will find Google Home users that can help you with some of your questions.

You can also find information on Google Home's social media accounts.

You can also request a call back from a Google Home specialist. You will have to be signed into your Google account to be able to do this.

Factory Data Reset

There are times when you will have to perform a reset. When you do a factory data reset, you cannot undo it once it is done. After you perform one, you have to setup your Google Home again and relink any smart home devices.

On your Google Home, press and hold the mute button located on the back of the device for 15 seconds. Your Google Assistant will confirm that you are resetting your Google Home device. There is no way to do this from the app.

Reboot

When you reboot your Google Home, you can fix many problems. There are two different ways you can reboot your Google Home.

From app:

1. All your devices need to be connected to the same Wi-Fi network.

2. Open your Google Home app.

3. Select the Devices icon in the upper right corner.

4. Scroll until you find the card for the device that you need to reboot.

5. Press the card menu icon and the select settings.

6. In the corner of the "device settings page" select the more icon and the reboot.

Google Home:

1. Unplug your Google Home's power cord.

2. Keep it unplugged for around a minute.

3. Plug your device back in.

Wi-Fi Problems

You may experience some problems associated with your Wi-Fi, or you may need to change the Wi-Fi that the device is connected to.

To change the connection:

Android:

1. Find the device card for your Google Home device; select the menu icon, then settings, and then Wi-Fi. The one listed is the one that you are connected to.

2. To switch it, scroll until you find the network that you want.

3. Enter the password for the network.

4. Select ok, and the Wi-Fi network will change.

iPhone

1. Find the device card you need and then select the menu icon, then settings, and the Wi-Fi.

2. To switch the network, select "forget this network" and the select "forget Wi-Fi network."

3. You will have to setup the device on the new network.

Made in the USA
Las Vegas, NV
04 December 2024

13354723R00085